The Flight to Freedom

By Allen A Vincatassin

DEDICATION

I would like to dedicate this book to Almighty God, my wife Joelle, my daughter Allena, and compatriots from Diego Garcia and the Chagos Islands.

CONTENTS

ACKNOWLEDGMENTS

It would have been impossible to write this book without the support of my wife Joelle.

I would also like to pay tribute to my late grandfather Michel Vincatassin, my late uncle Simon Vincatassin, my uncle Joseph Robert, and Selmour Cherry. Thank you for always supporting me, believing in me, and encouraging me every step of the way.

Special mention must also be made of the pioneering group who embarked with me on this life changing journey. Without them, there would be no story to tell.

My special thanks to Alan Vincent who helped me with the corrections of this book.

Above all, I must especially thank Almighty God for all He has done to lead and guide us on this improbable mission. Without Him we would never have succeeded.

1 EXILED

I was born on the island of Diego Garcia in the British Indian Ocean Territory. Looking back now, it's hard to believe that the day I was born, I was already destined to live in exile in a foreign land.

In 1966 the Government of the United Kingdom agreed to allow the United States Government to use the island of Diego Garcia as a military base. The agreement included provision for the forced removal of the indigenous people from the island. The United States feared opposition from the civilian population which could jeopardize their plans for a strategic long-term military presence on the island.

As a result, we, the indigenous people of Diego Garcia, were secretly and forcibly removed from our homeland and sent to live in Mauritius and the Seychelles. In addition, we were precluded from ever returning to the place of our birth, despite being British Subjects at the time of our eviction from the Island. The British Government decided to not relocate us to the United Kingdom so as to avoid embarrassment and ridicule should the news of our illegal treatment leak into public domain.

Their decision may also have had something to do with the fact that, at the time, we did not speak English, and were of a different ethnic group. The Governments of Britain and the United States regarded us as expendable but in God's eyes we were not. He had a marvelous plan for us.

Try to imagine being uprooted like a plant from the soil; wrenched from your ancestral and cultural heritage, and then transported against your will to a foreign land. Imagine living in the open without any provisions of shelter, food or employment. This is precisely what happened to us. We were forcibly removed from Diego Garcia on a ship called Nordvaer, and unceremoniously dumped on the wharf in Port Louis on the island of Mauritius in 1971. I was only one year old at the time.

Since this fateful event, my grandfather (Michel Vincatassin) has found it impossible to recover from being dispossessed of his rights as an indigenous citizen of Diego Garcia, and forced to live in a foreign land against his will. But his part in this story has to be told. While still on the island of Diego Garcia, he asked his employer to write a letter stating that he was being forced to leave the island against his will. Because of his foresight and courage, this document later formed the basis of his legal actions in the United Kingdom where he sought restitution and remedy on behalf of his disenfranchised people. Although illiterate, he had enough resolve to stand his ground and fight back.

With the help of his Nephew Christian Ramdas he managed to meet with Sir Charles Gaetan Duval, a renowned Mauritian Barrister at that time who took an interest in the case. In 1975 Mr. Duval instructed Bernard Sheridan to sue the British Government on the grounds that my grandfather had been coerced and compelled to leave his homeland against his will. My grandfather demanded his right to return to Diego Garcia, to be reinstated in his employment, and compensation of eight million pounds sterling.

Mathew Parris, a journalist of renown, revealed what had happened to the people of Diego Garcia in the newspaper. A man by the name of George Champion appeared before the British Parliament, asking the question "Who is Diego Garcia?" A subsequent documentary known as 'World in Action' interviewed my grandfather along with other members of the Diego Garcia community. The program was eventually aired on British television.
Slowly but surely the story unfolded in the British media. The cat was now out of the bag.

However, the matter was still treated as secret by the British Government as it had not yet been declassified. As a result, the case simply dragged on in the High Court in London. But media pressure was coming to bear, especially since a report had been published by John Madeley of 'Minority Rights Report'. He too had now joined the quest for justice.

In 1982 the British Government eventually decided that the matter needed to be resolved. Despite the fact that our initial claim against them had been for compensation of eight million pounds sterling, they agreed to pay four million pounds with the proviso that my grandfather withdraw his case before the High Court. He refused. Some members of the Diego Garcia community exerted pressure on him to agree to these terms and accept the settlement. He again refused on the basis that the proposed financial settlement was insufficient. Paul Raymond Berenger a Mauritian politician at that time, accused my grandfather of being obstructive and delaying payment of the claim.

I remember these events as if they happened yesterday. I recall, for example, how our family was threatened with violence if my grandfather refused to accept the settlement. There was a lot of confusion, tension, and uncertainty in our community during this time. This was exacerbated by the pressure of poverty and debt as individuals and families became increasingly desperate for financial compensation.

The threats became so extreme, that we eventually had to ask for police protection at our home in Roche Bois, a suburb of Port Louis. In addition, there was a protest before the British High Commission and the Mauritian Parliament. This was followed by the police brutalizing certain members of our community. The Mauritian Government came under ever-increasing pressure, and a solution to the problem had to be sought quickly to avert further civilian unrest.

Late one afternoon, while playing outside my house, five black cars suddenly appeared. Burly men streamed out of the cars asking for my grandfather. They said they had been sent to escort him to the office of the Prime Minister.

My Father (Joseph Vincatassin) accompanied my grandfather as they were whisked away in one of the cars. That evening my grandfather explained that he had signed documents authorizing the withdrawal of the case, and that the documents had already been transmitted electronically to the United Kingdom. He explained that the unrest in Port Louis, which had escalated into full-blown riots, had become untenable and dangerous. Under pressure from the local government, he had agreed to withdraw the case to prevent further unrest and bloodshed. He also stated that he felt as if he had now lost his personal freedom for a second time. He was being held to ransom by his own people who continued to threaten his life should they not get the money offered as part of the legal settlement. It seemed to him that they were unwilling to hold out for further negotiation which could have resulted in a better deal for the community.

This action sealed our fate. The British and Mauritian Governments entered into a bilateral agreement. Britain agreed to pay the four million pounds sterling into a trust fund, and Mauritius agreed to provide portions of land to the Chagossian community living in Mauritius at the time. The British Government asked the Mauritian Government to procure signatures from our people. In so doing, they would renounce their right to ever return to their homeland, and certify that the compensation of four million pounds sterling represents full and final settlement of their financial claims against the British and Mauritian Governments. Sadly, the signatures were obtained. Most of the compensation subsequently paid to the community, was used to settle personal debts that had accrued over a long period of time. Some even had to sell off the portions of land donated to them by the Mauritian government simply to survive. The only two person who refused to renounce their rights at that time were Simon David Vincatassin and Francois Louis; they did not take the last part of their compensation.

2 EDUCATION IS KEY

During the forced removal from Diego Garcia, my mother and father became separated. My mother Maryline, went to the Seychelles with her mother, while my father sailed to Mauritius. I on the other hand, had become separated from my parents, and was taken to Mauritius by my grandparents who assumed responsibility for me. This all occurred when I was only one year old. Little did I realize at the time that it would take seventeen years before I would be reunited with my mother.

My childhood in Mauritius was painful. I was constantly in tears. Why could I not be with my mother and father?. I simply wanted to be like other children who enjoyed a normal life. Although my grandparents (especially my Grandmother Marcelle Immouche) did their best to love and care for me, it could not heal the emotional wounds I felt. My grandmother lavished me with affection and my grandfather tried to inspire me as much as possible. My grandfather worked hard as a labourer and grave digger to make ends meet, and to provide me with a good education. Despite their love and support, I found school life very difficult. Not only did I feel abandoned by my parents, but soon realized that my illiterate grandparents could not help me with my studies.

In addition, I never regarded myself as a Mauritian while growing up in exile. I identified strongly with my heritage. I was constantly humiliated at school where locals ridiculed us as outsiders to their community. They knew that we came from the 'islands' and they labeled us 'Ilois', which means "islander". We were treated like outcasts - a people without identity.

As a result of this constant ridicule, I became increasingly bitter towards the British people for what they had done to us. It was because of them that we had been forcibly evicted from our homeland and were now unable to return. I found the whole experience very difficult and painful and could not accept the unrelenting malice shown towards us. However, in the midst of all this doom and gloom in my life, I realized the importance of getting educated. I instinctively knew that education would unlock the doors to my future success. I already had Britain in mind as a future destination because by now I had become aware that I was a British Subject. I would therefore have to learn to speak English if I intended living in Britain in future. My school taught English as a compulsory subject and it became clear to me that I could not fail in this subject if I wanted to attain my bigger goal.

At the end of my third year at London College in Port Louis Mauritius in 1984, I was forced to change college as a result of not doing well in English and other subjects. I concluded that I had neglected my studies as a result of playing too much during my free time. I started attending Bradley College in Long Mountain. It was situated in a village, and although the building was not as modern as in Port Louis, the school employed very good teachers. We also had the benefit of free extension classes every morning. I found these classes very helpful and they birthed in me a new enthusiasm for learning. The Principal of the college Mr. Ramchurn was also very encouraging. As a result I took a great interest in English as a subject and managed to attain good marks in my examinations.

In 1988 I entered my first job as a security guard for a company called Mauriguard. Being only eighteen at the time, I considered myself fortunate to find employment. I subsequently applied to become a policeman, but was refused the position because I did not have a Mauritian Identity Card. I was extremely disappointed but continued working in security to provide for myself.

I then decided to start a business and established a cleaning and gardening services company. But fierce competition and adverse circumstances put me out of business. A severe drought in the region made my life a misery and impacted very heavily on my fledgling business. One of my clients refused to pay me for the work I was doing for him because his grass was not green. Without money to pay my workers, I contemplated suicide. "Allen, only God can remove you from this situation" said my Sister Priscilla. As she spoke to me, it felt as if I was being punched in the chest. Something came over me and by the time we parted company, I just knew that God would deliver me from this terrible situation. Until this point in my life, I had always believed that God existed. But I had never had a personal encounter with Him. With my new found faith in God, I immediately returned to appeal to my client to pay what he owed me. Mr. Sharma became very agitated with me that evening. I was surprised to see him rushed into another room, and re-appearing minutes later with a cheque for five thousand rupees. I left the house rejoicing and praising God because I realized that I had just witnessed a miracle! I immediately committed my life to Jesus Christ and resolved to follow God's way and plan.

3 THE PURPOSE

We all have a purpose in life. But we need to discover that purpose. I had not yet discovered mine. So far, my life had been very difficult. Despite facing several defeats and setbacks with some of my plans and projects, I resolved to move forward with my newly discovered faith in God. I sometimes doubted whether my life had any purpose at all. So far the answer had eluded me but I continued to press forward.

By now I had developed a great interest in reading and studying the Bible. I enrolled myself onto a Bible study course at the Full Gospel Church of God. This is where I learned the principles of faith from Pastor Cyril Demba. It really opened my eyes! I started to realize that faith extends beyond my limited abilities and understanding. Faith was the key to help me get the breakthroughs and miracles I needed in my life. I realized too that many people do not believe in miracles. But I could no longer deny their existence as I had already witnessed them occur in my own life. After completing the Bible study course, I started to preach the gospel of Jesus Christ until I became a Co-Pastor of a local church. My involvement in the church gave me even more opportunities to witness the healing and saving power of God at work in our congregation.

I later worked alongside the Senior Pastor Marslin Feyande who preached the gospel in a way that people could easily understand. This humble servant of the Lord gave me money every Sunday so I could return home after church. Once again I had the benefit of witnessing the transforming power of God at work in the lives of the congregation. I was then presented with an opportunity to minister in South Africa, Seychelles and Rodrigues island.

Although I witnessed the miracles in the lives of others, I still struggled financially and concluded that something was missing in my relationship with God and my understanding of faith. I knew that there was a mandate from God over my life, but was confused as to why I was still struggling in these areas. However, I resolved to follow Christ and joyfully continued my duties as a minister of the Gospel.

Then one evening I was reading Proverbs 31:8-9 which says, ' Speak up for those who cannot speak for themselves, for the rights of all who are destitute. Speak up and judge fairly; defend the right of the poor and needy.' I should not have been on that particular page in my Bible because I was preparing a sermon about the Holy Spirit. I read the verse several times, and it really got my attention. I started praying, asking God if He was trying to tell me something important. Soon a discussion between the Holy Spirit and I ended in a disagreement. Once I realized that the Lord was asking me to become a spokesman for my disenfranchised people, I resisted the idea in every way. There were many reasons for this. I knew that the people could be very difficult to deal with. Secondly, I was already a Pastor and did not want to get involved with additional leadership responsibilities, especially politics!

But the more I protested, the more the Lord rebuked me. He then encouraged me, showing me examples of the lives of Moses, David, Jeremiah and Jesus Christ. I realized that they represented leaders whom God had chosen to fulfill His plans and purposes at various times. Each of them possessed unique leadership qualities that God used to advance His kingdom. I finally got the message and agreed to commit my life to God's plan for me, and to fulfill his greater purposes.

I soon realized though that I would meet with resistance from various people who already headed up various campaigns in our community. But I knew the Lord had spoken to me, that He would be with me, and that He would open doors of opportunity for me to speak on behalf of my people. My reluctance soon dissipated as I realized that God had connected me with my life purpose, and that anything that I would accomplish in future, would be attained only by faith in the One who sent me. Where I had previously only seen impossibility and adversity, I now began to realize that with God all things are possible to those who believe. Although there would be difficulties along the way, I was resolute in my newly discovered calling and purpose.

Soon afterwards, I received a call from my Cousin Spencer Vincatassin who worked in France at the time.

He asked if I would be interested to travel to Britain to follow the judgement of Regina –v– Secretrary of State for the Foreign and Commonwealth Office and Another, ex parte Bancoult; Admn 3-Nov-2000. The outcome of this case would determine whether or not we would be allowed to return to our homeland Diego Garcia. I responded positively because I already knew that this was the just the first of many doors that God would open for me in future. My cousin managed to speak to Mr. Georges Wuethrich who at the time was the Chairman of the Swiss Committee Of Support For the Chagossians in Switzerland. This resulted in them paying for me to travel to Switzerland and the United Kingdom so that I could follow the outcome of the case closely.

4 THE RIGHT OF RETURN

I eventually arrived in Switzerland in October 2000. The cold weather was mitigated by a very warm reception from Georges and his wife Nicole. They did everything they could to make me feel welcome. It soon became clear to me that they were very committed to our cause. Georges knew the history of events leading to our exile, and was investing his own time and money into our cause.

On the second of November we flew to Britain from Geneva along with my cousin Spencer. We spent the night at the Alhambra Hotel in London so that we could arrive at the High Court in good time to hear the judgement the following morning. Everything hinged on this High Court Judgement, as it would determine whether or not we would ever return to our place of birth.

The next day, we were in high spirits and full of hope. On arrival at the High Court we were met outside by a host of media representatives. Some of our compatriots had already made their way into the courtroom. They had linked up with Mr. Olivier Bancoult the leader of the Chagos Refugee Group in Mauritius. He had initiated the judicial review of our case against the British Government and was now present to hear the outcome of the review. Mr. Bancoult was represented by Sir Sydney Kentridge, and the British Government by Mr. Pannick. After a lengthy deliberation Mr. Justice Laws LJ and Gibbs J, ruled in our favour, quashing section eleven of the British Indian Ocean Territory Immigration Ordinance of 1971. The judge ordered the Commissioner of the British Indian Ocean Territory to write a new ordinance that would allow us to return to our homeland. The atmosphere in the courtroom was electrifying! We were ecstatic, to say the least, and greatly relieved that the court had finally ruled in our favour.

But our ecstasy soon turned into agony. Although the judge had ruled in our favour, he had not explicitly stated that we were free to return to the island of Diego Garcia immediately. I conferred with my friend Georges and my cousin Spencer, pointing this out to them.

Not only had we not been given the right to return to the islands immediately, but the Commissioner of the British Indian Ocean Territory would first have to promulgate a new law that would authorize us to return to the island at some time in future.

Meanwhile, everyone in the courtroom was jubilant. Richard Gifford the solicitor who had assembled a very good legal team for the case, was also very happy. He had followed the course of our struggle and had patiently and persistently worked to rectify the injustices we had suffered at the hands of the British Government. At the time he was still working for Sheridans, the legal firm that represented my grandfather's first legal action in 1975. By now, Olivier Bancoult and his fellow members of the Chagos Refugee Group, were eagerly relaying news of their 'victory' to friends and families in Mauritius outside the High Court. Cameras flashed as Mr. Bancoult displayed the V for victory hand sign to the press.

But our mood had changed. Beside me I heard Georges say quietly yet urgently "Allen, get your birth certificate out right now. This is your opportunity to tell the world that we are still not free to return to our homeland despite this so-called favorable judgement." I extricated my birth certificate from my coat pocket while being photographed by the press. Suddenly one of the journalists asked "What do you make of this judgement sir?" I calmly but firmly stated that unfortunately the judge had not ruled that we were free to return to our homeland Diego Garcia immediately.

My discussion with the journalist caught the attention of some members of Olivier Bancoult's entourage. They mistakenly thought that I was trying to rain on their parade. Immediately someone threatened me, claiming that I had spoken out against Olivier Bancoult in a newspaper article in Mauritius. They were referring to an article that Eshan Dinally wrote before I had even left Mauritius for Geneva. When Georges's wife Nicole heard the accusation against me, she angrily retorted, "Allen has a right to speak - let him do so." I responded by explaining to Olivier Bancoult that their accusation against me was baseless because the newspaper article in question did not levy any criticism against him.

Suddenly a young Englishman beside me said "I am from BBC World sir. Is it possible that you could talk with us in our studio which is not far from here?" Georges encouraged me to go, so we both headed for the BBC studios at Bush House nearby. While waiting to be interviewed we realized that by now the news of the outcome of the case would already have spread like wildfire throughout the media. Suddenly the journalist appeared to escort us to the studio. Armed with only a BBC visitor sticker on my jacket, I prepared for my baptism of fire in a UK radio station studio.

I was strangely at peace. I felt confident and assured that I had the right to express my opinion publically about this High Court Judgement. Before I knew what was happening, the interviewer asked me, "What do you make of this great victory in the High Court today on the right of return of your people to Diego Garcia?" I replied "The judgement is certainly a step forward, but it does not allow me to return to Diego Garcia today".

The following day we returned to Geneva armed with a few newspaper cuttings which had been handed to us by the owner of the Alhambra Hotel in London. We were very apprehensive as we pondered on the implications of our bitter-sweet victory. There I was on the front page of the Guardian holding my birth certificate; it was almost as if the page represented a new page in my future. Progressively, God started to pave the way for me to become a spokesman for my people. By now it had also dawned on me that our right to return to Diego Garcia may be further jeopardized by the presence of the US military base on the island. About a week later we received a copy of the new law that had been promulgated by the Commissioner of the Territory. It confirmed my worst fears. The new law stipulated that we could return to all parts of the territory (the outer Islands of the Chagos Archipelago) except the island of Diego Garcia. Obviously this had everything to do with the presence of the US military base which had been established on the island for strategic military reasons. Meanwhile, there was short lived jubilation in Mauritius. Many people thought that we had won the case, that they would now be compensated for their losses, and that millions of pounds would soon be coming their way. But this was not to be.

While in Geneva I was given the opportunity to represent our people at group sessions where legislation for the rights of indigenous peoples was being drafted. For the first time I found myself addressing an audience at the United Nations. In my first speech I explained that we had been exiled by the British Government, and that we are not Mauritians as they claim. The Mauritian representative tried to object to my statement, but the chairman of the meeting prevented her from interfering any further in the proceedings. I then subsequently met with several representatives from various countries, sharing our predicament with each of them.

 In addition to all this, I quickly had to become computer literate so that I could correspond and communicate more effectively with my ever-expanding sphere of influence.

I returned to Mauritius full of enthusiasm, focusing on the objectives that I wanted to achieve on behalf of my embattled community. I also realized that there was still the difficult task of having to tell them the truth about the real implications of the High Court ruling. I promptly called for a gathering of family members and friends, and explained that an imminent return to Diego Garcia was not possible. We then decided to establish the Diego Garcia Island Council. When our opponents discovered this, they branded me a dissident, claiming that I was trying to divide the community. But this backlash against me only made me even more determined to become a voice for my people.

5 THE DIEGO GARCIANS

A solid foundation is fundamental to the strength of any building. If the foundation is weak, what is constructed upon it, will fall. The foundation that I decided to build upon was that of my identity as a citizen of Diego Garcia. After all, I was born on the island of Diego Garcia and no one could deny that fact. My identity was inextricably linked with the place of my birth.

The 'Minority Rights Report' by John Madeley and the documentary 'World in Action' during the eighties reinforced my identity as a Diego Garcian. The title "Chagossians" emerged in the nineties, but it still did not help with the matter of being granted the right to return to the place of our birth. Despite the fact that 'Chagossians' could now return to the islands, we were still prevented from returning to Diego Garcia specifically, despite it being part of the Chagos Archipelago.

Sparks flew when I first started referring to myself as a Diego Garcian. I was now using a title that others from Diego Garcia were not using. Some felt that I was being divisive, but I was simply affirming the fact that Diego Garcia is an integral part of the Chagos Islands and that I too am a citizen of the Islands. Despite a barrage of criticism, I persisted in this manner.

My first meeting with the press in January 2001 did not go well. Journalists in Mauritius claimed that I did not know what I was talking about. A week after that one journalist name Henry Marimootoo stated that the Diego Garcians did not get their right of return but only those Chagossians of the outer islands that originated from Peros Banhos, Salomon islands and others. This is what had been published in the Mauritian press. My second press conference was now causing a stir in Mauritius because we were claiming that we too were Chagossians, and if this was the case, we too would have to be given the right to return to Diego Garcia. As a result of our news conference, those of the Diego Garcian community started to align themselves with our organization.

But this development was met with new opposition. One night the leader of the Chagos Refugee Group and I had a big argument about the matter on the phone. As the news of our claims circulated, my informants revealed that threats were being made against me by various parties. At this time, our party enjoyed only a small following and I realized that this alone placed us in a vulnerable position. Clearly I was the underdog. Soon various meetings were organised by our opponents who attempted to discredit my family and I. I refused to pay any attention to what others were doing, determined that I would remain focused on our key objectives. My fellow Diego Garcians simply had to win the battle to return to their homeland. There was no alternative.

I decided then that we would beg to differ with Olivier Bancoult and the British Government. As a result, we rejected the court ruling that permitted a return only to the outer islands. By now the majority of the Diego Garcian community had rallied around us as news of our actions quickly spread. We initiated contact with the British High Commission in Mauritius, stating our dissatisfaction in the matter of the High Court ruling, while making various representations on behalf of the disenfranchised members of our community. I now regarded myself as a British Diego Garcian rather than a Mauritian Chagossian. I wanted nothing further to do with the Mauritian Government. As a result I was branded a powerless dissident, while Olivier Bancoult was affirmed.

Despite the ongoing opposition, I knew I was on the right path. The peace of God governed my heart and my emotions and my faith continued to grow day by day. I spent a lot of time praying and standing on the promises of God in the Bible and was inspired by the stories of Moses, Nehemiah, David and Jesus Christ. The words of my grandfather also encouraged me greatly. At times when I feared for my life, I decided to put my trust in God because He had promised me that no weapon formed against me would prosper. Although there were still mixed feelings in the community about the stance I had adopted, the terrible truth about how we had been treated, was coming to light. As long as we remained steadfast, we would prevail.

But ongoing rumours about possible compensation made it difficult for me to move forward. Despite the fact that we were in continuous discussions with various representatives of the British Government, we were not yet involved in any legal representation on behalf of our people. In addition, the British Government had sidestepped the issue of compensation.

Despite various setbacks, our movement continued to go from strength to strength. Initially we were assisted by Mr. Selmour Cherry, a former member of the Ilois Trust Fund, who a good understanding of our struggle. We subsequently also received additional support from Charlesia Alexis – the 'Iron Lady'.

The British Overseas Territories Bill was introduced in the House of Lords in October 2001. The bill gave British Subjects living in the British Dependent Territories of the United Kingdom, right of abode in the United Kingdom. News of this development soon reached the ears of Sir Satcam Boolell, the Mauritian High Commissioner in London. He made some comments about the danger this bill posed to the Mauritian Governments' claim to sovereignty over the Chagos islands. In addition, rumours started to circulate that the Mauritian Government had lobbied British politicians to ensure that we would not be included in the amended bill. I called an urgent meeting of our party and committee members. We would have to prepare for a campaign to fight for our right of abode in the United Kingdom because we were now in grave danger of being marginalized even further. Our only hope was to be granted the right to remain in the United Kingdom legally, since we had already been denied the right to return to our homeland. Furthermore, the British Government was not interested in paying more compensation. We resolved to voice our opinion by protesting in the British High Commission, demanding that we be granted full British Citizenship with the right of abode in the United Kingdom. Charlesia Alexis and her friends went the extra mile and supported us greatly by partaking in the protest for days on end.

The rumours that had come to our attention, presented us with a rare window of opportunity. The British Government had been conducting a study to explore the feasibility of our return to the islands. We had no idea what the outcome of that study would be, but what we did know was that, in the interim, we had been prevented from returning to our homeland. Our only hope now was to start a new life in Britain, and that depended on whether or not we could achieve success in the British Parliament.

At this time I had knowledge of other community splinter groups that were very close to the Mauritian Government. Either we would have to consolidate to present a united front, or remain in abject poverty. As we planned to stage the protest, we were fully aware of the risks involved. We had no permission to stage a public protest, and risked arrest and prosecution under the Public Gathering Act. Our viewpoint was that we had nothing to lose.

Our stance was simply that if were unwilling to take any risks, we would land up with nothing. I was prepared to go to jail if necessary. I had no choice but to stand resolute alongside my fellow countrymen because I too had been illegally evicted from the place of my birth. There was a lot at stake and I instinctively knew that we were making the right decision.

On 13 March 2001 twenty two of us marched into the offices of the British High Commission and squatted in the Visa section. The High Commissioner refused to communicate with us. Our unexpected appearance in the building caused quite a stir. We displayed placards stating "We want our full British Citizenship now" while protesting peacefully. To our surprise, about twenty minutes after the protest started, we received a visit from the Assistant Commissioner of Police Mr. Jean Bruno. Mediation had begun! Finally, late that afternoon, the British High Commissioner agreed to communicate with the Foreign Office regarding the matter. We were then given permission to camp outside of the building for three days and nights. We enjoyed the ongoing support of Mr. Fernand Mandarin from the Chagos Social Committee, who also came and camped with our members.

On the third day of our protest we received an invitation from the Foreign and Commonwealth Office in London to attend talks. I subsequently had the privilege of leading a delegation to Britain, along with Ghislaine Louis, Irene Naraina, and Charlesia Alexis. At our meeting in London the British Government provided us with a guarantee that we would be granted British Nationality with right of abode.. Eventually, on 26 February 2002, the British Overseas Territories Act was promulgated and we became British Citizens with right of abode in the United Kingdom.

6 DECISION TIME

It was such a relief and a blessing to become a British with right of abode in the UK. We had won this battle. The day the news came, some people in our community who were pro-Mauritius, sang 'God Save the Queen' in front of the British High Commission. But I decided to not join in the celebration. Many of those around me did not understand why I responded this way. To them, I appeared ungrateful. But what had the Mauritian Government ever done for me? I still had no freedom to return home. Neither had the government of Mauritius done anything to prevent our exile in the first instance, or attempt to provide for us when we arrived destitute in Mauritius. Furthermore, successive Mauritian governments only had one interest; to obtain sovereignty over the Chagos Islands in order to benefit economically from the United States military presence on Diego Garcia. I was only interested with my next action plan.

I knew that my time had come. I resolved to spend a lot of time in prayer. I read my Bible for many days, seeking God's wisdom and inspiration. I needed even greater faith for what lay ahead of me. My God given life purpose was now beginning to manifest before my eyes. After seeking the Lord, I called a committee meeting and informed them that it was time for us to move to Britain to start a new life. Once we had reached our destination, we would continue the campaign to return to our beloved homeland. The meeting became chaotic as various committee members bombarded me with questions about how this plan could possibly succeed and how we would manage to survive abroad. Not being able to answer all their questions at the time, I felt quite embarrassed. I did not even know how I (let alone a group of people) would get to Britain, as I personally had no money to do so. Although I knew we were heading in the right direction, I had to come up with answers.

So I went to the British High Commission and asked them to get in touch with the Foreign and Commonwealth Office to ask for some help in this matter. The British High Commissioner had many questions and stated that it would be extremely difficult, if not impossible, for us to live in Britain. Mr. David Snoxell the High Commissioner, tried to convince me to abandon my plans by telling me that his own son, who lived in Britain, was unemployed. I suddenly realized the enormity of the task ahead of me. It's one thing coming up with big ideas, but another to execute them. At the time, we had very little insight into our options in Britain. But once again, faith arose in me.

I will never forget the day I received an invitation from the British High Commission to a farewell reception of the of the High Commission. Before leaving to attend the event, I fervently prayed that I would meet a representative of the Indian High Commission. My prayer was immediately answered! That evening, I met with just such a person. I thanked him for the support his government had given us by the late Indira Gandhi, who was at the time the Prime Minister of India. He handed me his business card and agreed in principle to meet with me again. It was only later that I realized that my meeting with this man had been divinely appointed because it triggered a series of crucial events that I could never have anticipated.

Weeks later, I visited the British High Commissioner's office in Port Louis to deliver some letters. To my surprise, the secretary told me that someone had called from the Indian High Commission, asking that I return their call as soon as possible. A shiver ran down my spine on hearing this wonderful news! I immediately returned the call and later that day had lunch with the same Indian government representative I had recently met. We then had another meeting during that week where I managed to discuss our plight in greater detail. My host asked me many questions. He appeared to be genuinely interested in our story, especially the outcome of the court case that now prohibited us from returning to our homeland. Once again, I took the opportunity to reiterate my gratitude for the way in which the Indian government had previously supported us. We then discussed the fact that my ancestry was linked to the southern part of India and it soon became evident that we had more in common than I had realized at first.

Now that we had established rapport, I felt at liberty to reveal my top secret plan to relocate my people to Britain.

It was time to make him privy to our plan which hitherto had only been discussed with those closest to me.

But before revealing the details of the plan, I asked for assurance that he would provide me with honest feedback as to our chances of success. I explained that I intended to relocate to Britain and start a new life there. I was of the opinion that this would open doors for my community as well. We had had enough of the abject poverty we were living in, and simply had to do something to improve our lot. I elaborated on my vision, explaining that the British Government had already demonstrated an unwillingness to assist us in any way. I concluded by saying that I realized the enormity (if not impossibility) of the plan and would like to hear his thoughts about our chances of success.

He retorted that if he were in my shoes, he would be reluctant to attempt it. He described it as a "very challenging step", and then went on to point out all the potential obstacles and difficulties we would encounter on route to our 'promised land'. He said that although he saw many challenges ahead, he believed we had a chance of success if we were determined enough. He then concluding by saying "I encourage you to move forward if that's what you have in your heart. If you need any help please do not hesitate to contact me. I'll be there for you.". It was like music to my ears. Waves of encouragement and strength welled up in my innermost being. This was the confirmation I had been waiting for! I realized too that God is no respecter of persons and that He can use anyone he chooses.

7 THE SUPPORT

The magnitude of this pioneering project suddenly dawned on me. Not only would my actions dramatically affect my future, but the lives of others, including future generations. News of my intentions would also raise the ire of anger my opponents once they heard of my plans to move to Britain. I felt sure that they would use this opportunity to discredit me even further.

I had already made peace with the British in my heart and no longer carried the burden of resentment. This meant that I could move forward without fear. I knew too that God would help me every step of the way.

The British government had closed every option available to us. Baroness Amos had already said that we would have to fend for ourselves and that no support will be forthcoming from their side. Despite the fact that we were free to return to the outer islands of the Chagos Islands, no provision had been made to permit any British Citizen coming from abroad, to settle in the United Kingdom. It was as if every bridge of hope had been destroyed. The gravity of the situation weighed heavily upon me as I realized once again how challenging this was all going to be.

But one morning, in the midst of the doom and gloom of our seemingly impossible situation, I had a vivid dream. In the dream, I found myself in what appeared to be a large cathedral or palace. Queen Elizabeth was seated on a throne and I was conducting music with a long staff in my hand. Alongside me stood a few of my compatriots. I was confused by the long staff that I held in my hand, thinking that it did not seem suitable for conducting music.

Suddenly I stopped conducting, the music stopped, and at that point the Queen stood up and made her way to a door. The door banged loudly. Startled, I awoke and jumped off my bed. I was very shocked by the dream because it all seemed so real! I prayed intensely that the Lord would help me to understand the meaning of the dream.

Days later I realized that the dream signified a divine mandate from God to proceed with my plan to relocate to the United Kingdom. God often speaks to people in dreams and visions and I had just had a divine encounter. This realisation boosted my faith to even greater heights. Suddenly I had no fear of the future because I now knew that my time had come and that I had to stand firm and act on my convictions. Soon after this dramatic event, I had a second meeting with my committee members. To my surprise, they were suddenly very positive about my proposals. Some individuals even expressed an interest in relocating to the United Kingdom themselves. The whole idea was now gaining momentum and I had to act quickly to fan the small flames of hope and interest into a raging fire. I subsequently met with the Deputy High Commissioner Richard Austen, who once again confirmed that the British government would not assist us in any way. Strangely, this did not bother me. He handed me a few pages entitled 'Moving to the UK' which I quickly read. The documents contained no references to support or assistance. Without hesitation, I asked Mr. Austen to inform Baroness Amos that we would be coming to the United Kingdom, with or without assistance from the government. Mr. Austen then suggested that I visit the Travel Care office located at the airport where I may be able to get further help and advice.

As news of our plan spread, my friend Jean Noel Bridiane arranged a meeting with a few people at the Caudan Waterfront in Mauritius. We made no mention of the meeting to the press, nor did we request permission from the Mauritian government. In my mind, this was now a British rather than a Mauritian matter. During this time my uncle Simon David Vincatassin, a former member of the Ilois Trust Fund, proved to be a great source of encouragement to me. Not only did he have extensive experience in working with our community, but he had also expressed his faith in me at various times.

I will never forget the day I visited Jes Travel on the ground floor of the British High Commission in Edith Cavell Street in Port Louis to inquire about flights to the United Kingdom. This was an aggressive act of faith on my part because I did not have the money to cover my own costs.

The owner of the agency Mr. Vic Acheemootoo was very sympathetic to our cause and agreed to assist in making arrangements for our journey. All those with me had enough money to pay for their own air tickets so Benjamin Laurent (who worked for the agency) proceeded to book one-way flights to Britain for seventeen people. But I still did not have the money for my own ticket.

I decided to make contact with a diplomat thinking that he may be able to help me. I called him to explain the predicament I was in and we agreed to meet at his office. Uncle Simon and I set out for the meeting while I silently prayed and gave thanks to God for success. On arrival at the office in Port Louis, I explained to my friend about my plan to travel to the United Kingdom. Without enough money to cover the cost of my air fare and a substantial telephone bill that was now due for payment, I could not go. "Not a problem my friend. I'll see what I can do for you" he replied with a smile. After making a few phone calls, he handed me all the money I had asked for! I rejoiced silently in my heart, knowing that God was with me and had just performed a miracle.

8 THE FLIGHT TO FREEDOM

There are times in life that we must be willing to do whatever is necessary to bring about a positive change in our circumstances. We have to leave our comfort zones, and be willing to forsake all - even those closest to us and the things we love most - so that we can embrace our future. This was such a time. We had arrived at our appointment with destiny and it was a point of no return.

On the afternoon of 15 September 2002, we set out for Sir Seewoosagur Ramgoolam International Airport in Mauritius. We were accompanied by friends and families from the suburb of Roche Bois in Port Louis. Eddy and Jean Philip Ramdas who had been involved in preparations for this historical event, were already at the airport to ensure that everything went according to plan. They had even prepared provisions of canned foods and drinks for us to take with us should we find ourselves stranded in Britain. We also had to undergo blood group tests prior to our departure. By now, some members of our entourage who possessed Mauritian passports, had been granted visitor Visas by the British High Commission as an act of goodwill. We were prepared for the worst, even if it meant spending our first few days in the arrivals hall of the airport in Britain. As we quietly but confidently pondered our fate, I was touched by the words of a song which said "When mountains fall, I stand by the power of Your hand". Approximately one hundred people had travelled to the airport to bid us farewell and it was a heart-wrenching moment as we finally took leave of our friends and families. Our entourage of nineteen souls was now ready and waiting to travel to Britain. These brave people were willing to risk everything to secure a better future for their families. They were Michael Vincatassin, Indra Vincatassin, Julie Botford, Max Botford, Guillano Soleil, Jennifer Soleil, Arlette Anamalay, David Anamalay, Patricia Herbu, Ricaud Herbu, Estelie Xavier, Jean Noel Narainen, Rudy Samoudy, Veronique Lafleur, Eddy Ramdas, Aniece Heviamoovima, Duesley Alexis, and myself.

But just as we started boarding the plane, I was stopped by the customs authorities. I nervously watched the rest of my party board the plane as my passport was taken from me. I still had an old British Dependent Territories Passport, while everyone else in my party had either a Mauritian or new British Passport. Because Mauritius had not recognized the formation of the British Indian Ocean Territory in the Chagos Archipelago, bearers of such passports often had difficulties with customs officials when travelling.

Anxiously I waited, not quite sure what was going to happen next. I thought back to Sir Charles Gaetan Duval. Because we were regarded as British Subjects, he had encouraged us to apply for our British Dependant Territories passports. I was among the first people in our community to apply for such a passport in 1985. Sir Duval had already declared his intention to fight for our right of abode in the UK. However, he then became a member of the Mauritian Parliament and the plan was subsequently abandoned.

My patience was quickly running out. As I sat waiting for what seemed like an eternity, dark thoughts crossed my mind. Were the immigration officials trying to prevent me from leaving the airport or were they delaying me on purpose so that I would miss the flight? Suddenly my travel agent came running towards me. Breathlessly she asked what was happening. I indicated that the authorities still had my passport which had been confiscated an hour ago. She assured me that she would not let the plane leave without me. She rushed over to the immigration counter to find out what was going on. I then saw her communicating with the aircraft by radio. Calmly she returned and stood beside me, assuring me that everything was under control. Fifteen minutes later the immigration officer returned my passport, apologizing for the lengthy delay. Suddenly I was being summoned to the departures gate over the public address system. I was so determined not to miss my flight to freedom that I sprinted to the departure gate. I boarded the aircraft amidst cheers and applause from members of my group already on board. I was greatly relieved as I realized that I had just overcome the final hurdle in Mauritius on my quest for a better life. A sense of great relief and elation came over me as I sat waiting to leave the place to which I had been exiled for so long. At the age of thirty two, I had many painful memories of Mauritius but I resolved again to pursue my future as a British Diego Garcian rather than as a citizen of Mauritius. My sojourn in Mauritius had provided me opportunities to make friends and to connect with my family.

I loved the Mauritian people but disliked the policies the Mauritian government had adopted towards my homeland. Consecutive Mauritian governments had come into power since the day we were dumped on the wharf in Port Louis. Each of these regimes had done nothing to assist us. Had it not been for divine guidance we would have remained in abject poverty. I had no remorse for my course of action, nor any sense of loyalty to a government that had treated us as second class citizens for so long.

After a few hours of flight we landed in Harare where we had enough time to browse through the duty free shop. After taking some refreshments, we promptly boarded our next flight to the United Kingdom. During the long flight, I again reviewed my plans. I felt the weight of responsibility for the group that had set out on a journey into the unknown with me. But I also realized that unless I handed this burden to the Lord, I would not succeed. After all – he had sustained me thus far and I felt confident that He would continue to do so. The decision had been made; we were going to declare ourselves to be destitute British Citizens on arrival in England. I recalled that during my last meeting with the Deputy High Commissioner Richard Austin, a leaflet he handed me mentioned that any destitute British Citizen arriving at a port or an airport in the United Kingdom, would be assessed by the local authorities to determine how they could be helped. Furthermore, I was now also armed with a letter from the British High Commissioner confirming that I was scheduled to have a meeting with the Administrator of the British Indian Ocean Territory in London. All my luggage had already been tagged with labels that displayed the address of the Administrator's office. If all else failed, we would simply camp at their doorstep.

9 IN THE REALM OF HER MAJESTY

Many of us seek to improve our lot in life. Millions of people are constantly migrating to what they perceive to be greener pastures. Difficulties such as warfare, unemployment, poverty, lack of education, racial conflict, exploitation and natural disasters, cause people to act in a manner that can only be described as self-preservation. This mass movement of people groups circling the globe in search of a better life, now dominates world politics. Nations are rising up against nations, and there seems to be a proliferation of violence and hatred worldwide. It seems that humanity is fighting for survival. This is precisely the situation we found ourselves in.

Our pursuit of justice on behalf of our disenfranchised people had always been conducted through peaceful means. I had always made it my duty to follow the way of peace no matter what. After all, Jesus demonstrated that peace is a very powerful weapon, and He set the perfect example for us to follow.

On the morning of 16 September 2002, at approximately six in the morning, we touched down at Gatwick Airport. I felt inner strength well up within me. Suddenly it was as if I was filled with energy – like a racehorse ready to bolt from the starting line. I had a race to run and this was the start of it. Everyone in our party was excitedly peering through the windows to get the first glimpse of our new home. This was where our future lay. The moment of truth had arrived and we were ready for it. By now my faith was rock solid and I knew that I had been born for such a time as this.

We were now in the realm of Her Majesty Queen Elizabeth II, the Sovereign to whom all the subjects of the overseas territories looked for protection and assistance. Previously we had been treated as expendable by the British government when the decision was made to lease the island of

Diego Garcia to the American military. Because the Americans did not want any civilians to remain on the island when they occupied it, we were simply evicted from our homeland without any thought for our future. This callous act represented yet another stain on the history of the United Kingdom.

Slowly the aircraft taxied to the arrivals terminal where it finally came to a stop. With bated breath we disembarked. But as we started walking down the corridor that connected the aircraft to the arrivals terminal, we were stopped in our tracks by a customs official. He started questioning my brother Michael, asking where he was going. We had just encountered our first obstacle in our promised land! I politely asked the officer if I could speak to him. He simply ignored me and continued questioning my brother. After being rebuffed a second time, I decided that it was time to take action. I firmly informed the office that he needed to address me as I was the leader of the group. Without further hesitation, I produced a letter from my jacket pocket while explaining that we were all British Citizens who had now come to live in the United Kingdom. I calmly said "You have no right to prevent us from entering the United Kingdom." The man appeared to be embarrassed once he had studied the letter and sheepishly told us to enter the arrivals terminal.

Once we had cleared customs and collected our luggage, we made our way to the arrivals hall. Many people were noisily greeting friends, family or business associates who had arrived on the same flight as us. We became quite emotional when we realized that there was nobody there to welcome us. Suddenly it felt very lonely in that large arrivals hall.

We then decided to position ourselves in a part of the arrivals hall of the South Terminal of Gatwick Airport that contained adequate seating, toilets, and shops that sold food. This would be our 'home' until we knew what to do next. By now we were already tired out from the long flight and the stress of not knowing what was going to happen to us. We decided to pray. I then laid down some ground rules as to how we should conduct ourselves at the airport. I also informed the group of what I planned to do next. Part of our entourage included a few members of our committee so I delegated some responsibilities to them for managing the group. Approximately half an hour later, I made my way to the Travel care office located nearby.

The officer on duty that morning was a woman in her late forties. I greeted her and said "I am here with seventeen of my fellow compatriots. We are destitute British Citizens who are stranded at the airport." She appeared to be quite shocked and stared at me intently. Moments later she asked how this had happened. I proceeded to explain how we had been sent into exile from our homeland in Diego Garcia to Mauritius, but that we now had a right to stay in the United Kingdom. I said that we had just arrived by plane from Mauritius, and that we had come to exercise that right. I continued to explain that the Foreign Office had refused to offer us any help or support, but that I already had a meeting scheduled with a government official. I then produced the letter which confirmed that a meeting had in fact been scheduled.

I could tell by the expression on her face that she was not quite sure what to do. She sympathetically explained that she was in no position to assist us in any way but that she would make some enquiries by phone. I asked for permission to use her phone and called the Administrator of the British Indian Ocean Territory.

A voice on the other end of the line answered "Charles Hamilton - how can I help." I calmly introduced myself as Allen Vincatassin. He asked where I was calling from. I proceeded to explain that I was at Gatwick airport with seventeen other people who had nowhere to stay. He sternly replied "Well, we told you that there would be no help on your arrival here. It's not my office's responsibility for what happens to you here, and there is nothing I can do." For a few seconds I stood in silence and then firmly replied "Well, I am afraid sir, you will have to do something about it. It was your office that removed us from our homeland in the first place, so it will be your office that will now have to sort this out. You do have a phone, so start making some calls. I will give you another call within the next twenty four hours. If you do not have a solution by then you will be embarrassed by what I reveal to the media." He retorted by saying "There is nothing I can do. You were expected to make your own arrangement before arriving here." My response was simply "You have twenty four hours sir", at which time I hung up the phone.

10 THE VICTORY

It was King Solomon who once said that the end of a matter is better than its beginning. I realized that we had met with a daunting obstacle that could result in us being stuck at the airport for a long time. It reminded me of Tom Hanks in the film 'The Terminal.' Hours passed as we sat waiting for something to happen. By now someone had given us a key so that we could use the airport bathroom which was a great help to us all.

Late that afternoon, the lady in the Travel Care office sent somebody to call me, saying that she had some news for us. She had managed to get in touch with an organization in Brighton which had the capacity to accommodate us. She promptly handed me the address and told me to make my way there along with the members of my group. I rushed back to break the good news to the rest of the group who were greatly relieved! We combined some of the money we had and headed for Brighton by train. After reaching Brighton late that evening in the dark, we were shocked to discover the condition of the property we were to stay that night. The building consisted of a dilapidated dormitory full of bunk beds. On our arrival the owner made some phone calls. About an hour later he informed me that Social Services was not prepared to pay him to accommodate us. Fear came over me as I heard this terrible news and by now I was wondering whether the lady at the airport had simply fobbed us off to avoid having to deal with the problem herself. It seemed that we had made a very big mistake by leaving the airport. When the owner realized that we had no alternative accommodation available to us, he called Social Services again. The Social Services official suggested that we return to Gatwick Airport, as we would at least be safe there. I convinced my group that we had no choice but to return to the airport. At least we had enough money to make our way back.

We were even assisted by some young people at the dormitory who helped us catch a coach back to the airport. It was almost as if we were refugees all over again. After a long trip of about an hour and a half, we arrived back at Gatwick airport, feeling quite exhausted after our ordeal. Despite the fact that security was tight at the airport because of the September 11 event, we managed to take refuge in the same place we had occupied earlier that day. We were so tired that we slept like babies.

The following morning we held another meeting to decide our next move. I suggested that we wait to see what would happen before executing the next phase of my plan. I returned to meet with the official at the Travel Care Office. To my surprise, another woman was in attendance. Once again I explained who we were and why we were here.

Time dragged on. By midday, nothing further had happened. By now a member of our group had managed to call family in Mauritius using the public telephone at the airport. Before leaving Mauritius, we had agreed to confirm our safe arrival once we had secured accommodation. The gravity of the situation was starting to take its toll on us. We had been in this state of limbo for two days already, not knowing what would happen next. Some in the group shed a few tears and this really touched me but I knew we had to be tenacious. We spent yet another night at the airport.

It felt as if we had been waiting at the airport for an eternity. I had a sense of foreboding but encouraged myself that good things come to those who wait. Early the following morning I prayed and encouraged myself further by reading the Bible. We conducted yet another meeting and I explained that I would now execute my next move. Straight after the meeting I returned to the Travel Care Office only to discover that no progress had been made since our last discussion. I decided to take matters into my own hands and again called Mr. Charles Hamilton. He was very aggressive and eventually I had to terminate the call. Just as I was about to leave the office a call came in on another line. It was for me! A strange voice on the phone said "Good morning sir. I am Mary Honeyman from Social Services of West Sussex County Council. I must apologize for taking so long to contact you. We did receive correspondence from the Foreign Office informing us that you were coming, but had no idea how to handle this situation, as this has never happened before. My priority now is to get all of you to a hotel. We will then assess your needs under the National Assistance Act of 1948." On hearing this news joy rose up within me and I suddenly felt ecstatically happy! I rushed back to the group to share the news of our victory. They hugged each other while shedding tears of joy. Arrangements were finally made for us to leave the airport later that day. We were finally accommodated at a Travelodge close to the airport. After being assessed by the Social Services team, we were provided with accommodation for six months, as well as a living allowance of thirty pounds a week. We had succeeded in our Flight to Freedom and this was the beginning of our new life.

ABOUT THE AUTHOR

Allen A Vincatassin lives in the United Kingdom with his wife Joelle and daughter Allena. He continues to lead his people by serving as the first President in exile for his country. In addition, Allen has been able to visit his homeland on various occasions. In February 2013 Allen persuaded the British government to undertake a pilot resettlement project which would enable his people to return to their homeland. Allen's life transforming story continues to be an inspiration to those who has heard it.

Notes

Everlasting

Printed in Great Britain
by Amazon